PICTURE
THIS
CENTURY

Front cover photograph:
The Constructors by Fernand Léger.
See page 23 for more details.

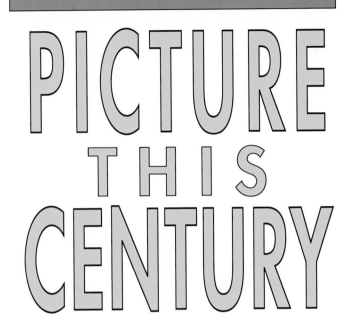

PICTURE THIS CENTURY

AN INTRODUCTION TO TWENTIETH-CENTURY ART

FELICITY WOOLF

A Doubleday Book for Young Readers

For Fintan, Ruairí and Samuel

Notes to the reader

The words in **bold** are explained in the glossary on page 36.
All measurements are given with height followed by width. Sculptures are measured by height only.

A Doubleday Book for Young Readers

Published by
Delacorte Press
Bantam Doubleday Dell Publishing Group, Inc.
666 Fifth Avenue
New York, New York 10103

Doubleday and the portrayal of an anchor with a dolphin are trademarks of Bantam Doubleday Dell Publishing Group, Inc.

This edition was first published in Great Britain in 1992 by Hodder and Stoughton Children's Books, a division of Hodder and Stoughton Ltd.

Library of Congress Cataloging in Publication Data

Woolf, Felicity.
        Picture this century : an introduction to twentieth-century art / Felicity Woolf.
            p.   cm.
        Summary: Surveys the subject matter and techniques used by various artists and movements in Europe and North America in the twentieth century, discussing such topics as cubism, abstract art, and pop art.
        ISBN 0-385-30852-3
        1. Art, Modern—20th century—Juvenile literature.
1. Art, Modern—20th century.   2. Art appreciation.
I. Title.
N6490.W66   1993
709'.04—dc20
                                        92-9128
                                          CIP
                                           AC

Printed in Italy

March 1993

10 9 8 7 6 5 4 3 2 1

PICTURE THIS CENTURY

AN INTRODUCTION TO TWENTIETH-CENTURY ART

FELICITY WOOLF

A Doubleday Book for Young Readers

For Fintan, Ruairí and Samuel

Notes to the reader

The words in **bold** are explained in the glossary on
page 36.
All measurements are given with height followed
by width. Sculptures are measured by height only.

A Doubleday Book for Young Readers

Published by
Delacorte Press
Bantam Doubleday Dell Publishing Group, Inc.
666 Fifth Avenue
New York, New York 10103

Doubleday and the portrayal of an anchor with a dolphin are trademarks of Bantam
Doubleday Dell Publishing Group, Inc.

This edition was first published in Great Britain in 1992 by Hodder and Stoughton
Children's Books, a division of Hodder and Stoughton Ltd.

Library of Congress Cataloging in Publication Data

Woolf, Felicity.
        Picture this century : an introduction to twentieth-century art /
Felicity Woolf.
                p.   cm.
        Summary: Surveys the subject matter and techniques used by various
artists and movements in Europe and North America in the twentieth
century, discussing such topics as cubism, abstract art, and pop art.
        ISBN 0-385-30852-3
        1. Art, Modern—20th century—Juvenile literature.
1. Art, Modern—20th century.   2. Art appreciation.
I. Title.
N6490.W66   1993
709'.04—dc20
                                                          92-9128
                                                            CIP
                                                            AC

Printed in Italy

March 1993

10 9 8 7 6 5 4 3 2 1

Contents

Introduction

Picture This Century introduces some of the many different kinds of art which have appeared in Europe and North America during the twentieth century. As well as paintings, these include sculptures made of steel, wood, ice, radio and television sets, and an old washing machine. This rather strange collection of materials shows how ideas about art have changed over the century.

In previous centuries there were accepted rules about what artists should paint or sculpt, and the materials they should use. During this century artists have learned to express themselves however they like. As a result, twentieth-century art is exciting to explore and often quite challenging to understand. Although only thirty works of art could be included in this book, *Picture This Century* should give you enough guidelines to look critically at any piece of art created in this century.

When you look at the photographs of paintings and sculptures in this book, always check the measurements printed near the illustrations. You may be surprised at the actual size of some of the works. At the end of the book there is a gallery list. This tells you where you can see the paintings and sculptures, if they still exist. Remember, there is nothing like seeing the real thing!

Until the end of the last century, it was taken for granted that an artist's job was to make paintings and sculptures look like recognizable people, places, and objects. After photography was invented, many artists began to question the meaning and purpose of art. If the camera could make an instant picture of the world, why should an artist do the same? Pages 8–21 of this book show how some artists developed new ways of painting and sculpting in answer to this question.

Some artists began to use color to express their own feelings, rather than to describe something realistically. Others began to show several views of one object at the same time, completely changing the way artists had shown space and volume in their paintings for the last four hundred years. One group of artists, the **surrealists**, painted their dreams and fantasies. (Words printed in **bold** are explained in the glossary on page 36.) These new approaches and experiments all emphasized the importance of the artists' own ideas and feelings.

By 1950 many paintings and sculptures were almost completely **abstract**. Artists working in this style became known as **abstract expressionists**. While most of the earlier experiments in painting and sculpture had taken place in Europe, the most famous group of abstract expressionists worked in New York (see pages 20–21). Many people believe that abstraction is the most important development in twentieth-century art and many artists still work in an abstract style.

But not all artists were satisfied with exploring only their innermost feelings. Some felt there were exciting experiences and new inventions special to the twentieth century that were known to many people and that should be explored through art.

Pages 22–27 show the way in which artists have considered three such subjects—war, work and industry, and women's position in society. War has seemed more terrible this century because of the invention of weapons of mass destruction. Work has changed for many people because of new technology invented to make modern products such as cars. Women's struggle to gain equal rights with men has been an important subject for many women artists.

Some of the artists in these central pages, such as Picasso in *Guernica* (page 25), used experimental styles. People often refer to paintings and sculptures made in these styles as "modern art." Other artists, such as Diego Rivera in his **mural** *The Making of a Motor* (page 22), used more traditional, realistic styles, because they wanted their work to be easily understood. It was the subject of Rivera's painting, rather than the style, that made it "modern" when it was finished in 1933.

The final section of *Picture This Century* introduces art of the last thirty years. In the first half of the century some artists broke new ground in the way they used color or showed space in paintings, or in the subjects they chose. But these artists still created paintings and sculptures that they expected to last, to be bought and sold, and to be put on show in private houses or in galleries. Much of the art being made at the end of our century breaks even these few rules.

The newest art is often temporary and made from unexpected materials. Some artists, such as Andy Goldsworthy and Christo (pages 32–33), make sculptures outdoors, which last only days or weeks and can now only be seen in photographs. Nam June Paik and Bill Woodrow (pages 31 and 34) make sculptures from old machinery. All these artists wish to communicate an idea rather than make a traditional, lasting piece of art.

One idea shared by several artists is a concern about the environment. We live in a world where we are always hungry for something new. The world's natural resources are being used up, and we produce huge amounts of waste that cannot be easily destroyed. Some artists in the final pages of *Picture This Century* try to make us think about these problems.

When you read *Picture This Century* the twentieth century will be nearly over. The book should help you look back at the ideas and interests that have inspired artists over the century. You may decide that there are big differences between art created at the beginning of the century and art being created today. For example, in 1913 Giacomo Balla celebrated cars and speed in a painting (page 13), while in 1981 Bill Woodrow showed his anxiety about the damage machinery does to the environment by making a "junk" sculpture (page 34).

But Balla and Woodrow have something important in common—the wish to create art that is completely different from anything made before. In previous centuries, when artists could use only certain materials and paint or sculpt traditional subjects, it was more difficult to be original.

In the twentieth century freedom from rules has meant that complete originality and rapid change is valued highly. This desire for difference is found in other areas of twentieth-century life—for example, in fashion and popular music. Thinking of it as something that links rather than separates each artist may help you to understand and enjoy the works of art in *Picture This Century*.

Color Run Wild?

At the beginning of the twentieth century some painters experimented with color. They believed that color in paintings should be personal to the artist, rather than realistic. These two paintings are examples of this view.

Until the invention of photography, painting a **portrait** was the only way to record someone's appearance. But by the end of the nineteenth century, the camera was taking over the portrait painter's job. Nevertheless, many artists believed that painted portraits could be more expressive and memorable than photographs.

In this portrait of his wife, Henri Matisse used vivid and strongly contrasting colors. He did not believe that Madame Matisse had blue hair, one yellowy-green and one pink ear, or a green stripe down her nose. But he wanted to show how color could be used by an artist in an imaginative and personal way, even when describing a face. The paint is not smoothly blended, and is applied quite roughly. Matisse wanted to create an interesting texture, emphasizing the special qualities of paint. The effect is very different from the even surface of a photograph.

Matisse liked the colors for themselves and the striking pattern of contrasts they made. He wanted Madame Matisse's dark hair to stand out against her pale skin. In portraits artists had usually painted white **highlights** on the forehead and nose. Matisse painted them green. The shock of this unexpected color draws us back to look

again at the picture. The green gives the face great power and personality, and the painting is usually called *Green Stripe*, rather than *Madame Matisse.*

Matisse exhibited this painting with others by some of his friends in Paris in 1905. The group was nicknamed the **fauves** (wild beasts) because of the shocking colors and rough textures in the paintings.

◄ 1. *Green Stripe*
(Madame Matisse)

Henri Matisse
1905
16 × 12¾ inches
Oil on canvas

2. *The Pool of London* ▶

André Derain
1906
25¾ × 38½ inches
Oil on canvas

The fauves also painted **landscapes** and **townscapes**. André Derain painted a series of pictures of London, many showing the river Thames. This painting is probably a view from London Bridge. You can see the Tower of London in the distance, behind the big ship in the **foreground**.

Like Matisse, Derain used color in a completely personal way. There are strong color contrasts, especially in the foreground—blue and orange, red and green, and red and blue. These vibrant colors make the foreground seem full of lively activity. Notice how paler blues and greens are used in the **background** to create a sense of distance.

Again, it is interesting to compare this style of painting with photography. Imagine a postcard of this river scene. How would it differ from Derain's painting? Which image do you think you would prefer?

9

Cubism: Different Points of View

The paintings on these two pages were painted in the style called **cubism**. The word cubism was invented to describe pictures in which the subject seems to be broken up into blocks or cubes. **Cubist** artists used many straight lines and right angles. The Spanish artist Pablo Picasso was one of the first artists to experiment with cubism.

This is a picture of a head, although it may take a little time to work it out. Think of the most important parts of a face and head—eyes, ears, hair, nose, mouth—and see how Picasso has drawn them. Can you see the five wavy black lines against white paint for one side of the hair and two black dots for eyes? What about a moustache, a pipe, and half a big bow-tie or scarf? Picasso has used a kind of shorthand to show them. They are all things that we see so often that we only need the simplest line or shape to recognize them.

Some of the parts of the head seem to be in the wrong place. The curved line, which is probably the man's left ear, seems to have slipped below the eyes. Some things can be seen from several points of view at once. For example, look at the pipe the man is smoking in the bottom right of the painting. The white paint gives the shape, sideways on, of a clay pipe; the black circle suggests the top of the pipe bowl, as if viewed from above; and the anchor hints at the name of the tobacco the man smokes!

If you turn to page 8 and compare Picasso's painting with that by Matisse, you will see that

Madame Matisse's head has been painted as if seen from one point of view. Although the colors are extraordinary, the shape of the head is normal. We also feel sure that Madame Matisse's head is solid, and takes up space. Picasso's painting is different. The lines and colors refer to the parts of a head, but the painting does not give any sense of the head taking up space. In other words, the head appears flat.

This idea of allowing a picture to look flat, instead of showing space and volume, was important at the beginning of the century.

Another Spanish artist, Juan Gris, came to Paris where Picasso was working, to find out about the latest ideas on art. In 1913 Gris went on a working holiday to Céret in the southeast of France, on the edge of the Pyrenees mountains. Can you make out mountain peaks, sky, fields, a farmhouse and small, round trees in *Landscape at Céret*?

Gris used bright colors, rather like Derain in *The Pool of London* (page 9). However, Gris's colors are probably closer to what he saw and are meant to suggest the intense heat of late summer at Céret. In his painting Derain shows things getting smaller toward the **background** to give an impression of distance. *Landscape at Céret* is divided into a pattern of irregular, upright strips. On these are painted small, broken patches of the landscape, which do not join up across the painting. This emphasizes the flatness of the canvas, rather than giving a sense of space and distance, as you might expect in a **landscape** painting.

As in *Head of a Man*, things are seen from different points of view. For example, look at the farmhouse in the middle of the painting. You can see some of the roof from above and a section of the wall from the side. Gris has included the parts

that struck him most vividly—the colored tiles, the white-washed wall, the dark, shuttered windows—rather than a complete picture of the farmhouse.

◀ **3. Head of a Man**

Pablo Picasso
about 1913
25¼ × 17½ inches
Oil on canvas

4. Landscape at Céret ▶

Juan Gris
1913
35¾ × 23½ inches
Oil on canvas

Toward Abstract Art

Like Matisse, Vasily Kandinsky believed that artists should use color freely, according to their imagination. This painting is called *Improvisation*. The word "improvise" is often used in connection with music. It means making up music as you go along. Kandinsky said that painting is like music. By calling this painting an "improvisation" he wanted to suggest that he let colors and lines take on shapes as he worked, without preplanning.

5. *Improvisation No. 30 (Cannons)*
Vasily Kandinsky
1913
43 × 43¼ inches
Oil on canvas

Music affects our feelings. Slow, quiet music makes us sad, while quick, loud, high-pitched music makes us feel lighthearted. Kandinsky said that colors act in the same way. Blue is tranquil and soothing, whereas yellow is exciting and unsettling. So, although some of the shapes here look formless, Kandinsky believed the colors would affect our moods. There are many extreme contrasts—black and white, blue and yellow, blue and red—and these are meant to have a disturbing effect.

Some people believe that Kandinsky was the first artist to paint **abstract** pictures, because he did not always use color and line to describe something recognizable. In fact, *Improvisation No. 30* is not a completely abstract painting. It is quite easy to pick out some shapes. Can you see the steep mountain with a red peak in the middle? And black lines suggesting houses and towers?

On the right at the bottom of the painting are two cannons with brown loops coming out of them. The cannons, slanting buildings, and bright, clashing colors are probably meant to make us think of war and destruction. The First World War broke out the year after this painting was made.

How could you paint a fast-moving car? Giacomo Balla hasn't included a car at all, but has suggested that something has just sped out of the right side of the painting. The curving lines sweep in that direction. The pink and some of the blue paint is very thin, as if the car has left a trail.

When you first look at this painting it might seem just a pattern of simple shapes. But if you look through the pattern you will see that the white area is a road, coming out of the green hills toward the **foreground**. Balla borrowed the idea of painting **landscapes** in simple geometrical shapes from **cubist** paintings (see Juan Gris's *Landscape at Céret* on page 11).

Balla belonged to a group of Italian artists called the **futurists**. The futurists noticed that cubist paintings rarely showed movement or the new inventions of modern life, such as the motor car. They believed that art should celebrate new technology, and experimented with ways of painting and sculpting movement and speed.

Balla's painting is called *Abstract Speed* because speed is something we can't really see. However, it is quite easy to connect the painting with something real—a fast-moving car. So is this a truly abstract painting?

6. *Abstract Speed
the Car Has Passed*

Giacomo Balla
1913
19½ × 25¼ inches
Oil on canvas

Revolution!

The period around 1920 was a time of great upheaval in Europe. The First World War had ended in 1918, while a great revolution was under way in Russia, where the Bolsheviks called on the workers to overthrow the Czar and fight for their freedom.

Artists were affected by the Russian Revolution and felt they had to respond to it in their work. Lyubov Popova belonged to a group of artists who believed that the revolution demanded a new type of painting. They had seen the work of artists such as Picasso and Giacomo Balla (pages 10 and 13) either in Russia or France, and thought that these artists had shown the direction art should take. At the same time they wanted new Russian art to rival and go further than the experiments of **cubism** and **futurism**. In **cubist** and **futurist** paintings objects, people, places, and machinery were still recognizable. The Russian artists made fully **abstract** paintings and sculptures.

Popova's painting does not show anything recognizable. It is one of many experimental paintings in which the artist explored different color combinations and overlapped various geometrical shapes. Triangles, rectangles, and circles appear to be laid on top of each other, creating a sense of space. Despite this layered effect the surface of the painting creates a pattern of balancing shapes and colors. A large black arrow-shaped triangle divides the painting. Blues, greens, and grays balance each other on either side. The straight lines and pointed forms suggest force and movement, which Popova thought appropriate for modern, revolutionary painting.

Popova taught at the training school for young artists set up after the revolution. At this school it was believed that students should study painting like a science, learning how to vary color, line, and texture and arrange them in different abstract compositions. Recognizable objects, places, or events were thought to be distracting and unnecessary.

◀ 7. *Abstraction*

Lyubov Popova
about 1920
13¼ × 9¾ inches
Watercolor and **gouache**
on paper

8. *The Bolshevik* ▶

Boris Kustodiev
1920
39½ × 55 inches
Oil on canvas

Not everyone in Russia agreed with these ideas. Boris Kustodiev was enthusiastic about the revolution, but thought that painting should be clear and easily understood by the workers. He continued to paint traditional scenes of Russian life.

The Bolshevik shows a **panoramic view** of the city of Moscow, covered in snow and swarming with workers, soldiers, and sailors, triumphant after the revolution. But Kustodiev has added something unrealistic—a giant Bolshevik strides through the streets with a huge red flag, which swirls behind him and wraps itself around the buildings in the **background**. Red was the color adopted by the revolutionaries, while the single figure sums up the strength and unstoppable momentum of the revolution.

Eventually, it was the way Kustodiev painted that was adopted as the official style of Soviet art. The abstract style developed by Popova and others was banned as too difficult to understand. The striding, powerful Bolshevik became widely used on posters and in the mass propaganda art of the Communist state.

Dreams and Disguises: Joan Miró and Surrealism

A carnival is a joyful celebration. People disguise themselves by dressing up and wearing masks, so that for a time they can pretend to be someone else. The Spanish painter Joan Miró wanted his painting to remind us of carnival time. The wavy lines and shapes suggest streamers, blowing in the wind. In the **foreground** two cats play with wool; their strangely colored faces and bodies suggest they are dressed up as harlequins. A yellow shape in the center at the top looks like a mask. Near this shape is a guitar and some notes of music. A blue and red circle seems to have eyes, a curly moustache, and a thin pipe. Can you find a fish and two exotic creatures with wings? You can probably recognize other things, too, but many of the shapes are mysterious and difficult to understand.

When Miró painted *Carnival of Harlequin* he was living in Paris. He knew a group of artists who are now known as the **surrealists**. They believed that art should not be simply pictures or sculptures of what we see in everyday life. Surrealist artists were interested in people's private thoughts and feelings. They said that dreams and memories should somehow be shown in art, because they are keys to people's personalities.

Some surrealist artists illustrated their dreams. In dreams, quite unexpected people and things turn up together. Sometimes this can be frightening, and there are surrealist paintings that seem to be based on nightmares. However, the atmosphere in Miró's painting is playful and relaxed.

Miró included certain forms in many paintings, such as the ladder on the left. The ladder doesn't go anywhere, but for Miró a ladder was linked with the idea of escaping from anything he didn't like, just as a carnival disguise can let someone get away from normal life.

Miró said that he jotted down ideas for *Carnival of Harlequin* when he was starving—so hungry that he began to see things that weren't really there. So the painting may be partly a record of these imaginary visions. The overall background of the painting is of two different shades of beige, one darker than the other; these suggest a floor and a wall, and on the right there is a window with a view of the sky and a mountain. It is as if in Miró's imagination the carnival has come into his room.

9. *Carnival of Harlequin*

Joan Miró
1924–5
25¾ × 36¼ inches
Oil on canvas

Sea Sculptures

When you first look at Alexander Calder's sculpture, you probably just see groups of different colored metal shapes and looped wire. If, however, you saw it in the Museum of Modern Art in New York, you would realize that the sculpture hangs from the ceiling, in a stairwell, so that all the parts move. Then the name of the sculpture, *Lobster Trap and Fish Tail*, might make you suspect something fishy! Perhaps the wire is a net or trap, the red, yellow, and black shape part of a fish, and the dark petal shapes parts of a plant. The movement suggests the gentle swaying of fish and plants underwater.

You may have seen or made a mobile at home or at school. Alexander Calder invented the mobile. The word means able to move. Calder wanted to make sculptures in which each part could move on its own, so that there was never just one view of the sculpture—it would always be changing.

The sculpture may look easy to make, but it was difficult to balance each section and allow each part to move freely. Calder was helped by being both a trained engineer and a brilliant mathematician.

10. *Lobster Trap and Fish
    Tail*

Alexander Calder
1939
101 inches
Wire and painted sheet
    metal

The "fish" and "leaves" of *Lobster Trap and Fish Tail* were cut out of thin sheet metal and then painted. This may not seem remarkable now, but in the 1930s when Calder invented this technique, no one had seen brightly colored moving metal sculptures before. Calder was a great friend of Joan Miró, and his mobiles have the same playfulness as some of Miró's paintings (see pages 16–17).

11. *Pelagos*

Barbara Hepworth
1946
14½ inches
Wood with color and
    strings

The title of Barbara Hepworth's sculpture is also important. "Pelagos" is Greek for *sea*. Until you know this, Hepworth's rounded wooden sculpture seems entirely **abstract**. But the title suggests you should link the shape and color of the wood—light brown on the outside and painted white inside—with the sea. Perhaps the sculpture reminds you of a wave, curling over as it hits the shore.

Barbara Hepworth lived by the sea at St. Ives in Cornwall, England. She said that the sweep of St. Ives Bay inspired her when she was making *Pelagos*. The sculpture is not meant to be a picture of the bay; rather it suggests the safe, protecting arms of the landscape.

The two curling ends of the wood are joined by strings. They are rather like the strings of a harp or a guitar, which must be kept at exactly the right length and tension to stay in tune. Without strings the wooden body of a musical instrument would be silent. In the same way, the strings of *Pelagos* make the wood seem strong and alive. Without them, perhaps the ends would uncoil and spring apart.

American Art After 1950: Big Is Beautiful

In an excavation you dig down to find things hidden underground. Looking at Willem de Kooning's painting *Excavation*, you can imagine that the artist has dug into, or scraped back, the surface paint to show black lines and colored patches underneath. It is impossible to make complete sense of the bones, scraps of pottery, coins, and other oddments found in an excavation. In the same way it is extremely difficult to put together these lines and shapes and work out exactly what they are. On the other hand, the blurring of some of the lines, the sharp angles and the impression of chaos in the painting, might suggest something about the artist's mood when he painted it. Do you think he was calm and tranquil, or angry and confused?

Willem de Kooning worked in New York, where, during the 1940s and 1950s, many artists experimented with new ways of painting. Many were Europeans (de Kooning was Dutch) who had come to the United States before or during the Second World War. They believed that they could make a truly modern and important school of American painting by developing European experiments in **abstract** and **surrealist** art. Look at the paintings by Picasso (pages 10 and 25— *Guernica* was shown in New York in 1939), Kandinsky (page 12), and Miró (page 17) to get an idea of the paintings the New York artists admired.

The New York group tended to use large canvases to give their work power and impact. Some believed that by painting freely and without knowing exactly how their compositions would work out, they could come closest to expressing their deepest and most personal feelings. This group of artists became known as the **abstract expressionists**.

◄ 12. *Excavation*

Willem de Kooning
1950
79½ × 99 inches
Oil on canvas

13. *Interior Landscape* ►

Helen Frankenthaler
1964
104¼ × 92 inches
Acrylic on canvas

Although Willem de Kooning is usually described as an abstract expressionist, his paintings are almost never completely **abstract**. In *Excavation* some of the black lines are a kind of shorthand to describe parts of the body. Can you pick out teeth, eyes, the curves of breasts, arms and legs? Do these intrigue you and make you want to keep looking at the painting? Or do you find them an irritating puzzle too difficult to work out?

This painting by Helen Frankenthaler is also very large; the artist used a technique known as **soak-stain**. There are big areas of thin color—black, yellow, purple, and green. At the bottom edge, part of the canvas has not been painted at all. There are no lines and almost no brush marks visible in the painting. The abstract expressionists believed that brush marks left on the canvas were important clues to the artist's personality, mood, and method of working. Frankenthaler's method of pouring the paint does not leave such evidence, but the title, *Interior Landscape*, suggests the painting is about an imaginary world known only to the artist. The painting takes us inside the artist's mind, just as de Kooning's title suggests digging into the artist's thoughts.

If a painting is called a landscape, we might expect to see space represented in it. Yet the soak-stain pouring of the paint makes *Interior Landscape* appear flat; we cannot look "through" to a distant view. Instead we see only undisguised paint. The artist teases us a little. The outside bands of color, the black and yellow, seem at first like a picture frame, but there is no "picture" in the middle. Pleasure in looking at the painting comes not from seeing a "view" but in the striking combinations of large areas of color.

Work and Industry

Many twentieth-century inventions have changed our lives. Think of cars, airplanes, television, and computers, to name just a few. Some of these are made in factories with the help of powerful machinery. Until recently most industries needed a large work force. Many artists have been excited by industry and technology, and some have explored the way humans are affected by them.

The earliest modern car assembly plant was the Ford works in Detroit, Michigan. The Mexican painter Diego Rivera specialized in large **murals**, and he was commissioned to paint a series of twenty-seven **frescoes** about Detroit industry. Rivera spent weeks in different parts of the Ford plant, studying the manufacture of the new Ford model V8. The two main frescoes show motors being made, and the assembly of the car body.

14. *The Making of a Motor* (detail), from *Detroit Industry*

Diego Rivera
1932–3
Dimensions of whole panel 17 ft 8½ in × 45 ft
Fresco

This detail, about 16 feet square, of one fresco, shows work on parts of the car engines. You can see earlier processes above, as the metal is cast into shape. But it is the car workers who have been painted in most detail. Rivera painted men of different races and ages working together harmoniously. Despite the hot and noisy conditions, the men are strong and dignified. Rivera emphasized the vital human work force, rather than the finished product. When the frescoes were finished, some people criticized him for being too sympathetic to the workers.

In 1913, the artist Jacob Epstein bought an industrial drill and was inspired by it to make this half-robot, half-human sculpture. At one time, the drill and its three supports formed the legs of the sculpture. The head takes the form of a sharp beak and visor, which hides the face. The jointed arms have no hands. There seems to be a baby inside the robot's body, one of the few signs that this creature is human. Is Epstein suggesting that a human being has been taken over by a machine and turned into a robot? Or is he celebrating the power that machinery gives to man?

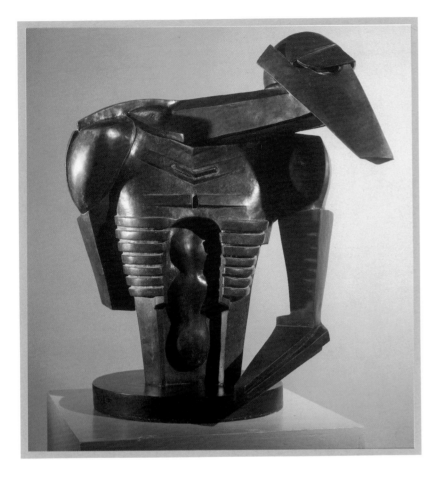

15. Torso from
The Rock Drill

Jacob Epstein
1913
27¾ inches
Bronze

16. *The Constructors* ▼

Fernand Léger
1950
117¾ × 78¾ inches
Oil on canvas

Would you expect the construction of an electricity pylon to make a good subject for a painting? Fernand Léger did! He believed that artists should help people to see beauty and excitement in the materials of modern life.

Léger was excited by the contrasts between the clouds, the construction workers, and the steel girders. The men and the clouds have soft, rounded outlines, while the girders are hard-edged and brilliantly colored. The men do not seem to strain heroically like Rivera's car workers. It is the steel pylon that Léger celebrates.

23

Artists and War

You have probably seen films about war. They often emphasize the spectacular side of action in battle. The paintings on these pages offer a different view. They ask us to think seriously about the tragedy and waste of war.

The main area of action in the First World War (1914–18) was in Belgium and France, but the conflict spread to Greece and Turkey. The British artist Stanley Spencer joined the Royal Army Medical Corps and was sent to Smol in Macedonia, northern Greece. Back home in England, he painted this picture of the wounded being carried on stretchers dragged by mules to a first aid center, set up in an old church. All attention is turned toward the bright light of the makeshift operating theater. This could have been a scene of great confusion and suffering, but instead there is order and calm. Most faces are hidden. Spencer believed that the wounded men had now found peace.

17. *Travoys Arriving with Wounded at a Dressing Station at Smol, Macedonia*

Stanley Spencer
1919
71¼ × 85 inches
Oil on canvas

Guernica is a town in the Basque region of Spain, which was bombed by fascist forces in 1937 during the Spanish Civil War. The town was totally destroyed and people who tried to escape were gunned down in the fields. The Spanish artist Pablo Picasso believed the bombing was a terrible act of savagery. A few days later, he began studies for a huge canvas about the suffering of the innocent victims of war.

In complete contrast to Stanley Spencer, Picasso wanted to emphasize the terror and pain the bombs caused. *Guernica* is not a realistic description of the incident. Although the bombing happened in the day, Picasso set his scene indoors, at night. He used only black, white, and gray. Only a few people are included, most of whom are women. Women and children are usually victims of war, rarely taking part in the fighting.

Picasso deliberately distorted and exaggerated those parts of the body that express fear. We see eight heads (human and animal) and their expressions very clearly. The mouths are open as if screaming and arms and hands stretch out in agony. The painting creates the dreamlike feeling of a nightmare, partly because of the strange way animals and humans are mixed together. On the left of the picture is a bull, who appears strong and unaffected by the suffering. Perhaps he is the spirit of Spain.

Faces are also a key to the painting *Vietnam (III)* by the American artist Leon Golub. His painting shows American soldiers and their victims in the Vietnam War, which took place in the 1960s and 1970s. Like *Guernica*, this is a very large painting. The faces of the American soldiers are painted in most detail, while the faces of the dead Vietnamese on the left can hardly be seen. The soldiers seem isolated and lost in their own worlds. They are drawn in different scales, so that we cannot work out a setting for the action. Most look away from their dead enemies as if distancing themselves from the killing. Four soldiers in the foreground are literally cut off by the edge of the canvas. Perhaps this suggests both the random destruction of war and the way the soldiers have become cut off from feelings of sorrow and pity.

▲ 18. *Guernica*

Pablo Picasso
1937
136¾ × 305 inches
Oil on canvas

19. *Vietnam (III)* ▶

Leon Golub
1974
119 × 332¾ inches
Acrylic on canvas

Women's View: Protest to Survive?

You may have noticed that there are not many paintings or sculptures by women in this book. Although women have always made things at home that require artistic skill, such as sewing and embroidery, these crafts have not been considered important in the history of art. To paint and sculpt in the same way as male artists, women needed to go outside their homes to be trained and find work. Until the second half of the century, it was difficult for a woman to do this. During the last twenty years more women than ever before have managed to be taken seriously as professional artists. Many of these women believe that their job is to show the problems that women face in everyday life.

Convicts and Lunatics is a poster made for the fight to give women the vote in Britain—a fight not completely won until 1928. The campaign to win the vote gave many women their first chance to make pictures that would be seen outside the home, usually embroidered banners and designs for printed posters. In this poster three types of people who did not have the right to vote are shown together—a prisoner, a madman, and a dignified woman who has been to college—all locked out by men. The artist shows how unfair it is to put an educated woman on the same level as the two men who can offer nothing to society.

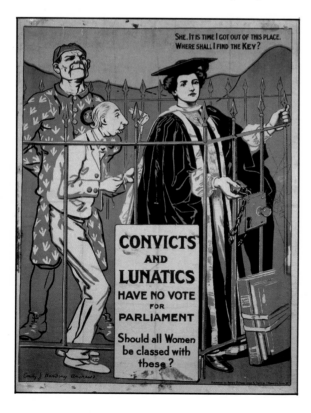

20. *Convicts and Lunatics*

Emily Harding Andrews
About 1908
39 × 30 inches
Color poster

Barbara Kruger is an American artist who lives in New York. Like Emily Harding Andrews and the **suffragists**, she wants as many people as possible to see her work. She believes that art does not have to be limited to paintings and sculptures in a gallery. This is a large billboard poster, placed where people expect to see an advertisement. A little girl points to a small boy's muscles. She is impressed by his strength. Heroes are traditionally strong—and violent. The writing suggests that man's strength is not necessarily something to be welcomed. What do you think passersby made of this?

▲ **21.** *We Don't Need
Another Hero*

Barbara Kruger
1985
119 × 238 inches
Billboard

22. *'She Ain't Holding
Them Up, She's
Holding On (Some
English Rose)'* ▶

Sonia Boyce
1986
85 × 38½ inches
Crayon, chalk, **pastel**, and
ink on paper

Sonia Boyce is a black artist living in England.
Black women artists have found it even more
difficult to survive as artists than white women.
Boyce's picture is about the balancing act she has
to perform. She ''holds up'' her respectable
family, suggesting she has to live up to their
expectations of her. Her dress bears the words
''Some English Rose,'' a phrase used to describe a
beautiful, white English woman. This is another
unjust expectation Boyce cannot live up to, for
many people will never consider her beautiful, if
beauty means being white. Sonia Boyce is asking
us to accept her for herself, as an artist and as a
black woman.

Pop Art

Who would ever have imagined that an artist would want to paint a picture of Coca-Cola bottles? In the 1960s **pop artists** made art out of all kinds of everyday things—food, packages, soda cans, advertisements, comics—in fact, anything that was popular and easily recognized. Pop artists believed that art should be about what everyone knows and experiences, especially in the big cities. They looked outward at modern life and rebelled against the idea that serious art had to be **abstract** and difficult for most ordinary people to understand.

In *Green Coca-Cola Bottles* Andy Warhol simply painted many times one of the most famous American products—Coca-Cola. Warhol was trained as a commercial artist and was fascinated by advertising. Advertisements are probably the pictures that most people know best. Yet *Green Coca-Cola Bottles* isn't the same as an advertisement, because it doesn't try to persuade you to buy. The Coca-Cola is just there—a part of everyday life, which we would hardly have noticed until Warhol pointed out its popularity. So in paintings like this one, Warhol shows that even trivial things are important in our lives.

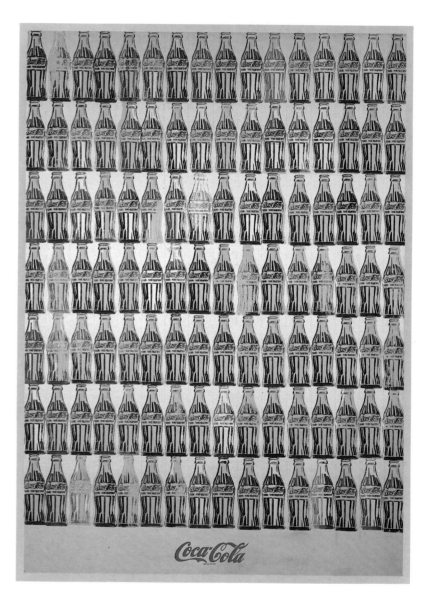

Some bottles are not as clear as others. They look as if they have been printed mechanically, and not hand-painted as was, in fact, the case. As part of his wish to shock and change ideas about art, Warhol always tried to make his work look as impersonal as possible, leaving no trace of brush marks or any other sign of how the painting was made. In many later works Warhol used printing techniques as an alternative to painting.

28

◀ 23. *Green Coca-Cola Bottles*

Andy Warhol
1962
81 × 56½ inches
Oil on canvas

▲ 24. *Whaam!*

Roy Lichtenstein
1963
67½ × 158¼ inches
Acrylic and oil on two canvases

It's easy to see what Roy Lichtenstein based this painting on. It is a hugely magnified page from a comic strip about war. It even includes the kinds of words you find in comics. This was Lichtenstein's way of rejecting **abstract expressionism** (see pages 20–21). Like Warhol, Lichtenstein used a technique that made the painting look printed. Areas of color were filled in with stenciled dots and outlined with thick black lines. Each step was carefully planned, and the artist knew exactly how everything would work out.

Why do you think Lichtenstein chose this image? Maybe he just enjoyed the shape and color of the explosion, and saw it as a kind of joke against the ''explosions'' of color in **abstract** paintings. But maybe he had a more serious idea. Violence is shown on television, in films, and in popular comics and magazines. We see so much ''pretend'' violence that we no longer think about the terrible reality of war or human destruction. Perhaps that is the point Lichtenstein is making.

What's the Great Idea?

Would you like to buy any of the paintings or sculptures shown in this book? I don't suppose *Felt Suit* would be your first choice! The German artist Joseph Beuys thought art was far too important to be bought and seen by only a few individuals. He believed that artists could use their creative power to affect the way people live and think.

Beuys was a fighter pilot during the Second World War. In the winter of 1943 his plane crashed in the Crimea, in southern Ukraine. He was rescued by local people, the Tartars, who revived him by covering his body with fat and wrapping him in thick felt made from animal fur, to stop heat escaping from his body.

Joseph Beuys made many "sculptures" about this experience using fat and felt. *Felt Suit* is a simple way of recalling the way felt saved his life. According to Beuys, sculpture, and all art, should be based on an idea that is of vital importance to the artist. This idea should also say something about the way human life depends on certain natural materials. Beuys was probably the first artist to use his work to make people think about the destruction of the environment. In one of his projects, he organized tree-planting in cities all over the world.

Maybe you don't think that what Beuys does is art. However, he has been very important to many artists in the last twenty years. He has shown them that artists do not have to limit themselves to working in a studio, making paintings and sculptures for sale. An artist can have much wider aims.

25. *Felt Suit*

Joseph Beuys
1970
73¼ inches
Felt

One of the aims of the Korean-born artist Nam June Paik is to make us think about modern technology and how it affects our lives. In 1986 he made a group of sculptures called *Family of Robot. Grandfather* belongs to this group. Do you think of robots as technically advanced computers that help human beings, or do you think of them as machines without feelings, which can threaten the human race?

If you imagine robots living in families, it makes them seem friendlier and more human. Perhaps they can experience feelings of love, anger, hope, and fear. It also means they are born, grow old, and die.

Can you see how Paik shows that *Grandfather* is old? He is made of out-of-date radio and television sets. His head is a vintage radio, while the rest of his body, arms, and legs are old television sets. Paik has given *Grandfather* life; a color video tape plays on new screens set into the old television cabinets.

Nam June Paik's work suggests many ideas. In this piece perhaps he is saying that while the latest technology quickly becomes outdated, the importance of human relationships and family life remains constant.

26. *Family of Robot, Grandfather*

Nam June Paik
1986
100¼ inches

9 vintage television cabinets, vintage radio cabinet, 11 new television sets, video cassette player, 30-minute Paik video tape

Nature into Art: Two Landscape Sculptures

Both artists discussed here make sculptures outside, in different kinds of landscape. The sites chosen by the artists are extremely important. For Christo, who made *Valley Curtain*, the site decides the shape, size, and color of the sculpture. For Andy Goldsworthy, the place he chooses provides the material for his sculpture, as well as its character.

Christo Javacheff is a Bulgarian-born artist who now lives in the United States and is known as Christo. In 1972 he succeeded in stretching a curtain of orange nylon, about 1,312 feet wide and 328 feet tall at its highest point, across the Grand Hogback valley at Rifle in the Colorado mountains. The nylon sheeting was hung from steel cable, which was also used to fix the bottom of the fabric to the ground. Although the steel structures took eighteen months to erect, the curtain itself was unfurled in a few minutes.

Many people helped Christo put up *Valley Curtain*, and they became caught up in the excitement of the project, perhaps feeling they were artists too. The sculpture was taken down after twenty-eight hours, because of high winds, and so now we only know what it looked like from photographs.

Christo sells drawings and models of his sculptures to pay for new projects. These have included wrapping a bridge in Paris in woven nylon material and surrounding eleven islands in Biscayne Bay, Florida, with over 6,456,000 square feet of pink fabric.

Why do you think Christo invents such extraordinary sculptures? Perhaps he believes that art should be like a fireworks display—beautiful and spectacular but soon over. Christo wanted people to be shocked and amazed by the size and color of *Valley Curtain* as they drove toward it.

27. *Valley Curtain, Rifle, Colorado*

Christo
1970–2
199,920 square feet
Woven nylon fabric
   and steel cables

32

He then wanted the sculpture to disappear quickly, so that the experience remained only in people's memories. It is as if in a world where there are few surprises, and where science can explain most things, Christo wanted to create something completely unexpected and breathtaking.

The British sculptor Andy Goldsworthy also works in the countryside. Like Christo's sculptures, his are short-lived and recorded in photographs. But in most other ways Goldsworthy's sculptures are very different.

When making sculptures in the landscape, Andy Goldsworthy usually works alone, building quite small pieces, and using only the materials he finds around him. His only tools are stones and pieces of wood, and he fixes things together with thorns, twigs, mud, or water. To make *Ice Arch* he cut slabs of ice, placed them over a pile of stones, and left them to freeze into shape overnight. The first three attempts didn't work, because the arch collapsed. Even the fourth arch, shown in the photograph, would have lasted only a few hours before melting.

A sculpture like *Ice Arch* is surprising rather than shocking, because it reveals the beauty in something ordinary and familiar. Goldsworthy wants to make people aware of the natural beauty around them, which he believes is threatened.

28. *Ice Arch*

Andy Goldsworthy
1982
no dimensions given
   by artist
Ice

Beaver and Bird: Real or Imaginary?

Have you ever used cardboard boxes, pieces of unwanted wood, or old baby carriage wheels to make something new? Many of Bill Woodrow's sculptures are made from old kitchen equipment that has been thrown away. This sculpture is still recognizable as a washing machine—you can see the knobs at the back and the inside workings. The front panel, apparently made of wood, has been partly cut away, and at first sight it seems to have been eaten by a beaver. When you examine the sculpture more closely, however, you see that the missing sections were cut away by the artist and used to make the beaver. And the panel isn't wood at all, but metal, covered in sticky-backed plastic, made to look like wood.

Bill Woodrow enjoys playing these kinds of tricks. But his sculptures are not just clever jokes; they also have a more serious meaning. Washing machines made a huge difference to ordinary people's lives at home. But all machines are made at least partly from natural materials and need energy to run, and we are now so dependent on machines that we are rapidly using up the earth's resources. We are also creating dangerous waste because when the machines wear out, we cannot or do not destroy them. In fact, old washing machines cannot be "eaten up," and our need for new ones destroys the natural habitat of animals like beavers.

29. *Twin-Tub with Beaver*

Bill Woodrow
1981
28¾ inches
Mixed media

We are not meant for a minute to believe that *Big Bird* is anything other than imaginary. It is one of a group of sculptures Niki de Saint Phalle called her *Skinnys.* You can probably guess why. The wings and body of the bird are pierced with holes, which make it appear light and airy and able to fly away. Although it is now in an art gallery, *Big Bird* was made to be seen outside in the garden. You should see grass, plants, and sky through the holes.

Unlike Bill Woodrow, Niki de Saint Phalle did not start with anything premade. Instead, she built a metal framework or skeleton in the shape of the bird. This is covered with polyester, a kind of liquid plastic that hardens and lasts well. *Big Bird* is painted in bright bands and patches of **acrylic**, which keeps its brilliance even if *Big Bird* is left outside.

Niki de Saint Phalle believes that birds are special. They often play an important part in legends, myths, and fairy tales. They rescue people, bring messages of hope, and provide food and comfort. In one legend, a bird (the phoenix) rises miraculously from the ashes of a fire. When Niki de Saint Phalle is working on a sculpture she feels as if she is in the power of a magical bird, which carries her off on an exciting journey to an unknown destination. In the same way, she wants her brightly colored sculpture to take us away from the everyday world into one of fantasy and imagination.

30. *Big Bird*

Niki de Saint Phalle
1982
62½ inches
Mixed media

Glossary

abstract a term used to describe paintings and sculptures that do not show anything recognizable

abstract expressionism the style of painting of the **abstract expressionists**

abstract expressionist an artist who creates **abstract** paintings, and shows his or her feelings by means of lines and colors and the way the paint is applied

acrylic paint in which the **pigment** is mixed in a chemical liquid, which dries much more quickly than oil and forms a tough, plastic film. First used from about the 1950s

background in a realistic painting the space is divided into **foreground**, middle ground and background. The background is the space farthest from the viewer; the foreground is nearest to the viewer.

cubism a movement in art that adopted the **cubist** style

cubist a style of painting that divides up the subject into simplified blocks and lines. These shapes are then shown in one painting or sculpture from several different points of view.

fauves French word meaning "wild beasts." Used to describe a group of painters who used bright color in a personal way, rather than realistically

foreground see **background**

fresco a method of painting on wet plaster

futurism the style of art of the **futurists**. It was based on **cubism**, but attempted to show movement.

futurists a group of Italian artists who celebrated the most advanced technology of the early twentieth century in painting and sculpture

gouache	paint made from opaque **pigments** mixed with water and glue
highlights	paint used to show the parts of an object or person that reflect most light
landscape	a painting of the countryside
mural	a wall painting
panoramic view	a view from high up so that you can see all around
pastel	soft, colored chalk
pigment	a colored powder, which gives paint its color
pop artists	artists whose work is about everyday objects, from comics and advertisements to soda cans and food
portrait	a painting that records a particular person
soak-stain	a method of pouring paint onto canvas. **Acrylic** paint applied in this way tends to soak into the canvas
suffragists	people who took part in campaigns to allow women to vote
surrealism	a movement in art. "Surreal" means "beyond reality," and **surrealist** art shows the importance of experiences that are hidden in normal life, such as dreams and memories.
surrealists	the group of artists who invented and developed **surrealism**
townscape	a painting of a town or city
watercolor	paint made from transparent **pigments** mixed with water and glue

Gallery List

1. *Green Stripe (Madame Matisse)*, *Henri Matisse* (1869–1954), Statens Museum for Kunst, Copenhagen, Denmark

2. *The Pool of London*, *André Derain* (1880–1954), Tate Gallery, London, England

3. *Head of a Man*, *Pablo Picasso* (1881–1973), Thyssen-Bornemisza Collection, Lugano, Switzerland

4. *Landscape at Céret*, *Juan Gris* (1887–1927), Moderna Museet, Stockholm, Sweden

5. *Improvisation No. 30 (Cannons)*, *Vasily Kandinsky* (1866–1944), The Art Institute of Chicago, Chicago, IL

6. *Abstract Speed the Car Has Passed*, *Giacomo Balla* (1871–1958), Tate Gallery, London, England

7. *Abstraction*, *Lyubov Popova* (1889–1924), Yale University Art Gallery, New Haven, CT

8. *The Bolshevik*, *Boris Kustodiev* (1878–1927), Tretyakov Gallery, Moscow, Russia

9. *Carnival of Harlequin*, *Joan Miró* (1893–1983), Albright-Knox Art Gallery, Buffalo, NY

10. *Lobster Trap and Fish Tail*, *Alexander Calder* (1898–1976), The Museum of Modern Art, New York, NY

11. *Pelagos*, *Barbara Hepworth* (1903–1975), Tate Gallery, London, England

12. *Excavation*, *Willem de Kooning* (1904–   ), The Art Institute of Chicago, Chicago, IL

13. *Interior Landscape*, *Helen Frankenthaler* (1928–   ), San Francisco Museum of Art, San Francisco, CA

14. *The Making of a Motor* (detail), from *Detroit Industry*, *Diego Rivera* (1886–1957), The Detroit Institute of Arts, Detroit, MI

15. Torso from *The Rock Drill*, *Jacob Epstein* (1880–1959), Tate Gallery, London, England

16. *The Constructors*, *Fernand Léger* (1881–1955), Musée National Fernand Léger, Biot, France

17. *Travoys Arriving with Wounded at a Dressing Station at Smol, Macedonia*, *Stanley Spencer* (1891–1959), Imperial War Museum, London, England

18. *Guernica*, *Pablo Picasso* (1881–1973), Prado Museum, Madrid, Spain

19. *Vietnam (III)*, *Leon Golub* (1922–   ), Collection of the artist. Courtesy Josh Baer Gallery, New York, NY

20. *Convicts and Lunatics*, *Emily Harding Andrews* (active 1877–1902), Artists' Suffrage League Poster, Fawcett Library/Mary Evans Picture Library, London, England

21. *We Don't Need Another Hero*, *Barbara Kruger* (1945–   ), temporary billboard at Hammersmith Broadway, London, England

22. *"She Ain't Holding Them Up, She's Holding On (Some English Rose),"* *Sonia Boyce* (1962–   ), Cleveland County Museum Service, Middlesbrough, Cleveland, England

23. *Green Coca-Cola Bottles*, *Andy Warhol* (1928–1987), Whitney Museum of American Art, New York, NY

24. *Whaam!*, *Roy Lichtenstein* (1923–   ), Tate Gallery, London, England

25. *Felt Suit*, *Joseph Beuys* (1921–1986), Workcomplex, Hessisches Landesmuseum, Darmstadt, Germany

26. *Family of Robot, Grandfather*, *Nam June Paik* (1932–   ), Collection of Robert Shiffler, USA

27. *Valley Curtain, Rifle, Colorado*, *Christo* (1935–   ), temporary sculpture, Grand Hogback, Rifle, CO

28. *Ice Arch*, *Andy Goldsworthy* (1956–   ), temporary sculpture, Brough, Cumbria, England

29. *Twin-Tub with Beaver*, *Bill Woodrow* (1948–   ), Collection Leeds City Art Galleries, Leeds, England

30. *Big Bird*, *Niki de Saint Phalle* (1930–   ), Hugh Lane Municipal Gallery of Modern Art, Dublin, Ireland

Acknowledgments

The Author's and Publisher's thanks are due to the following for supplying photographs:

Albright-Knox Art Gallery, Buffalo: 9; Jeanne-Claude Christo and Christo (photograph by Harry Shunk): 27; © The Detroit Institute of Arts, Detroit: 14; Fabian Carlsson Gallery, London, England: 28; Hugh Lane Municipal Gallery of Modern Art, Dublin, Ireland: 30; Leeds City Art Galleries, Leeds, England: 29; Leon Golub, collection of the artist, courtesy Josh Baer Gallery, New York: 19; Mary Evans Picture Library/Fawcett Library, London, England: 20; Moderna Museet, Stockholm, Sweden (Statens Konstmuseer): 4; Musée National Fernand Léger, Biot, France: 16; Novosti London Picture Library: 8; Museo del Prado, Madrid, Spain: 18; Rump Collection, Statens Museum for Kunst, Copenhagen, Denmark: 1; San Francisco Museum of Modern Art, San Francisco, gift of the Women's Board: 13; Tate Gallery, London, England: 2, 6, 11, 15, 24, 25; The Art Institute of Chicago, Chicago: 5 Arthur Jerome Eddy Memorial Collection 1931, 12 gift of Mr. and Mrs. Noah Goldowsky and Edgar Kaufmann, Jr., Mr. and Mrs. Frank Logan Purchase Prize Fund, 1952, all rights reserved; The Artangel Trust, London, England: 21; Collection, The Museum of Modern Art, New York: 10; The South Bank Centre, London, England: 22 collection of Cleveland County Museum Service, 26 collection of Robert Shiffler; Thyssen-Bornemisza Collection, Lugano, Switzerland: 3; Trustees of the Imperial War Museum, London, England: 17; Whitney Museum of American Art, New York: 23; Yale University Art Gallery, New Haven, CT, gift from the Estate of Katherine S. Dreier: 7.

The Author's and Publisher's thanks are due to the following copyright-holders:

ADAGP, Paris and DACS, London 1991: 2, 9, 10; Andy Goldsworthy: 28; Barbara Kruger: 21; Beth Lipkin: 15; Bill Woodrow: 29; Jeanne-Claude Christo and Christo: 27; DACS 1991: 1, 3, 4, 5, 12, 16, 18, 24, 25; Imperial War Museum: 17; Leon Golub: 19; Mary Evans Picture Library/Fawcett Library: 20; Nam June Paik: 26; Niki de Saint Phalle: 30; Novosti Information Agency (NIA): 8; Sir Alan Bowness: 11; Sonia Boyce: 22; © 1991 The Estate and Foundation of Andy Warhol/ARS NY: 23.

Index

This edition published by Parragon Books Ltd in 2014 and
distributed by

Parragon Inc.
440 Park Avenue South, 13th Floor
New York, NY 10016
www.parragon.com

ISBN 978-1-4723-8240-5

Printed in China

THE EMPEROR'S NEW CLOTHES

Retold by
Katherine Sully

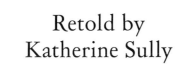

Illustrated by
Deborah Allwright

PaRragon

Bath • New York • Cologne • Melbourne • Delhi
Hong Kong • Shenzhen • Singapore • Amsterdam

Once there was an emperor who was very proud of how he looked.

More than anything, he loved new clothes. He bought the finest silk and satin, velvet and lace, and he kept the royal tailors busy day and night, making new clothes.

They even made matching outfits for the emperor's little dog.

The royal closets were overflowing!

Every morning, the emperor would admire himself
in the mirror and say,

"Aren't I the best-dressed emperor in the whole wide world?"

No matter what they really thought, everyone around him
would bow and say, "Yes, Your Majesty, you are."

Every year, the emperor led a royal parade through the city, wearing his very best clothes. But one year, he decided that even his best clothes would not do.

"This year," he told his tailors, "I want to wear an outfit so splendid no one will ever forget it!"

The tailors worked day and night making the best clothes they could fashion. They brought the emperor piles and piles of new clothes to try on. But nothing pleased him.

"These clothes are much too ordinary, I must have something much **more magnificent!**"

The tailors kept trying, but the emperor was still not happy. At last he told his chief minister, "Find me some new tailors, who can make truly magnificent clothes!"

The chief minister set out at once. As he walked through the marketplace, he overheard two men talking to a well-dressed couple.

"We are the best tailors in the land," the first man was saying.

"Yes," the other agreed. "We make clothes so fine that no one in the whole world has ever seen anything like them!"

The chief minister rushed over.

"You must come with me to the emperor's palace," he told the tailors.

The chief minister brought the two tailors to the emperor.

"Can you make clothes that are truly magnificent?" the emperor asked them.

"Oh, yes, Your Majesty," they replied. "When people see our clothes, they never forget them!"

"What is so special about your clothes?" asked the emperor.

"They are made from a rare and wonderful cloth," the first tailor explained, "and only we know how to weave it."

"That sounds perfect!"

exclaimed the emperor.

He gave the tailors a bag of gold and promised
them more when the clothes were finished.

The two tailors were given their own workshop, where no one would disturb them. They quickly went to work.

A few days later, the chief minister came to see how they were doing. The tailors seemed to be very busy—but the chief minister could not see any cloth.

"Our cloth is very fine and delicate," the first tailor explained. "See how it shimmers in the light."

"Only a fool cannot see this beautiful cloth," said the second tailor.

The chief minister did not want the tailors to think he was a fool, so he said, "Yes, it is very beautiful indeed."

The tailors pretended to snip off a piece of cloth, then carefully fold it up. They handed it to the chief minister, who took it straight to the emperor.

"Only a fool cannot see this wonderful cloth," said the chief minister, handing the invisible cloth to the emperor.

The emperor did not want anyone to think he was a fool, so he quickly said,

"Yes, it is the most beautiful cloth I have ever seen!

Give the tailors more money, and tell them to work more quickly!"

A week later, the chief minister went to see the tailors again.

They seemed to be hard at work, cutting and pinning their invisible cloth.

"What do you think of the cloak we are making?" asked the first tailor.

"Only a fool would not be able to see how beautiful it is!" said the second tailor.

Because he did not want to look like a fool, the minister replied, "It is the most splendid cloak I have ever seen. I am sure the emperor will be pleased!"

At last, the day of the parade arrived. The emperor eagerly went to his dressing room, where the tailors were waiting.

Very carefully, the tailors helped the emperor put on his wonderful new clothes.

Of course, the emperor could not see any clothes at all! But he didn't want the tailors to think he was a fool, so he said,

"These are the most magnificent clothes I have ever worn."

Smiling, he admired himself in the mirror.

Wearing nothing at all, the emperor made his way down the grand staircase, through the great hall, and out to the palace courtyard.

Everyone bowed as the emperor passed. No one noticed that he wasn't wearing any clothes!

The parade made its way through the city.

Crowds of people stood in the streets, cheering and clapping, waiting for the emperor to appear.

When they saw the emperor at last, they could
not believe their eyes!

The people began to whisper to one another.
But no one had the courage to say anything out loud.

One little boy and his sister made their way
to the front of the crowd.

As soon as they saw the emperor, they
began to laugh and point at him.

"Look!" they giggled. "The emperor has no clothes on!"

And everyone, even the emperor himself, knew it was true.

Filled with shame, the emperor made
his way back to the palace to get dressed.

"Look!" they giggled.
"The emperor has no clothes on!"

And everyone, even the emperor himself, knew it was true.

Filled with shame, the emperor made
his way back to the palace to get dressed.

"I have been **very** foolish," he said to his chief minister.

"If my appearance had not been so important to me, I would never have let myself be cheated by those two tailors. I will never be so vain about my clothes again."

He was true to his word—and he was a much happier emperor from that day on.

The End